THE GREAT ARTISTS

Henri Matisse

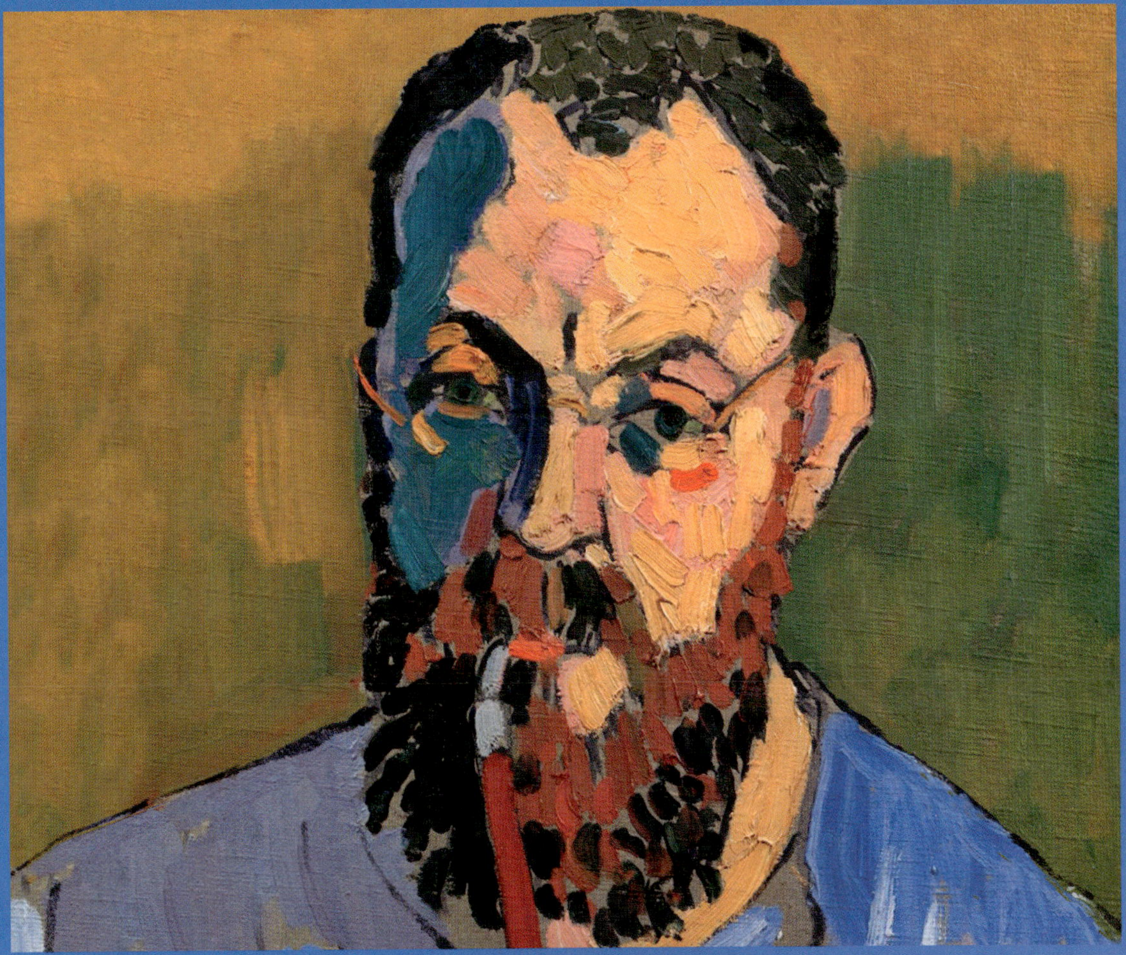

Anjali Raghbeer

Om KIDZ
An imprint of Om Books International

'Henri, Ooooh! Look at this coffee pot. It's beautiful,' gushed Amelie. Monsieur Chocolatière was not pleased being bought as a wedding present and stared at Henri, a tall man with a serious face and a black, long beard, as he poured hot coffee from M. Chocolatière's spout.

'Hello! Hello!' M. Chocolatière turned. 'Did you know that I am the reason Mr. Matisse knew he was going to be a painter?

"From the moment I held the box of colours in my hands, I knew this was my life." That's what Mr. Matisse said.'

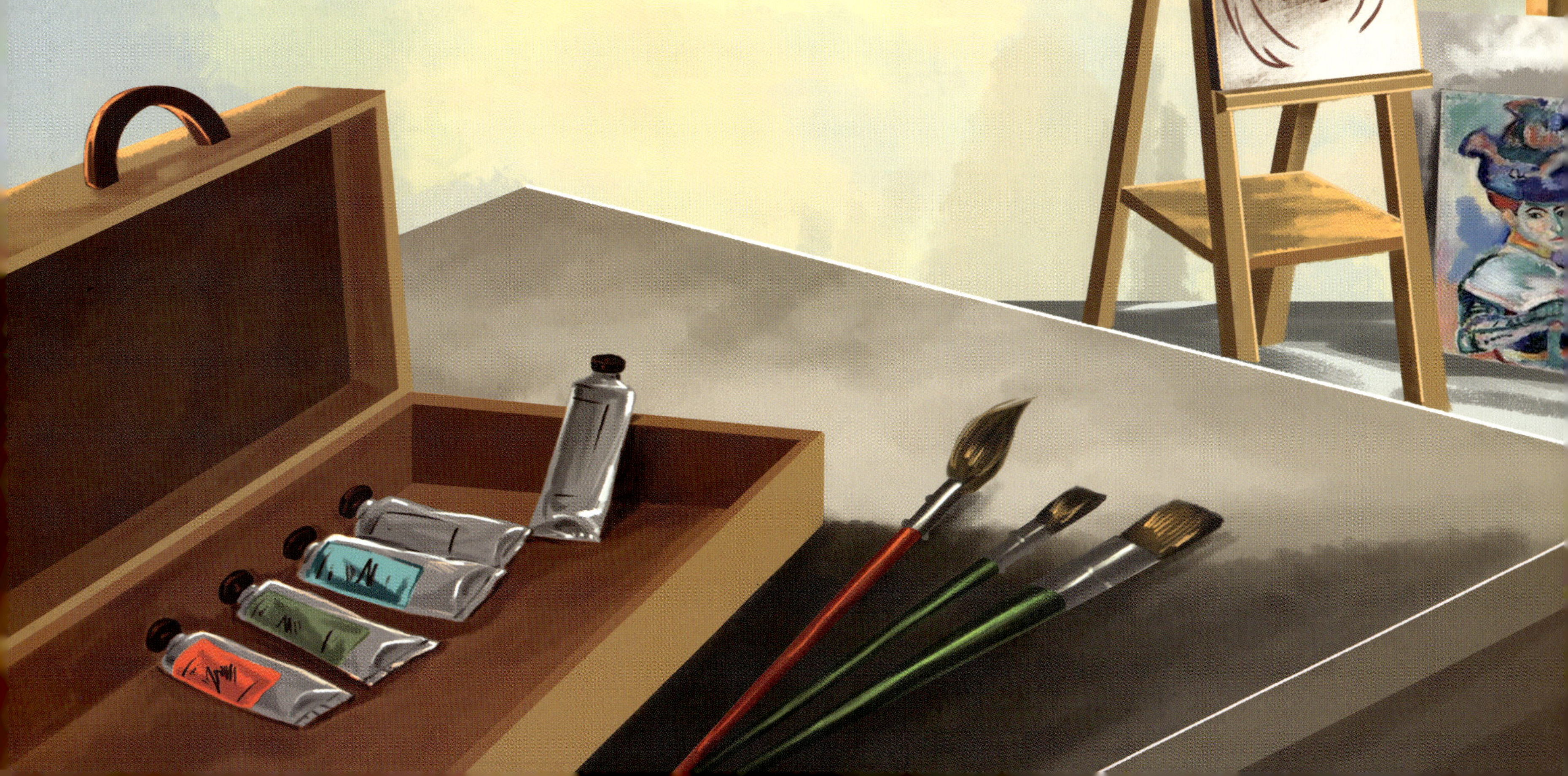

'You know, when he fell ill, his mother got me as a gift for him,'said Miss Paint-box. 'I've been with him ever since.'

Mr. Matisse obviously enjoyed painting objects.

'I wonder if he will paint me,' wondered M. Chocolatière.

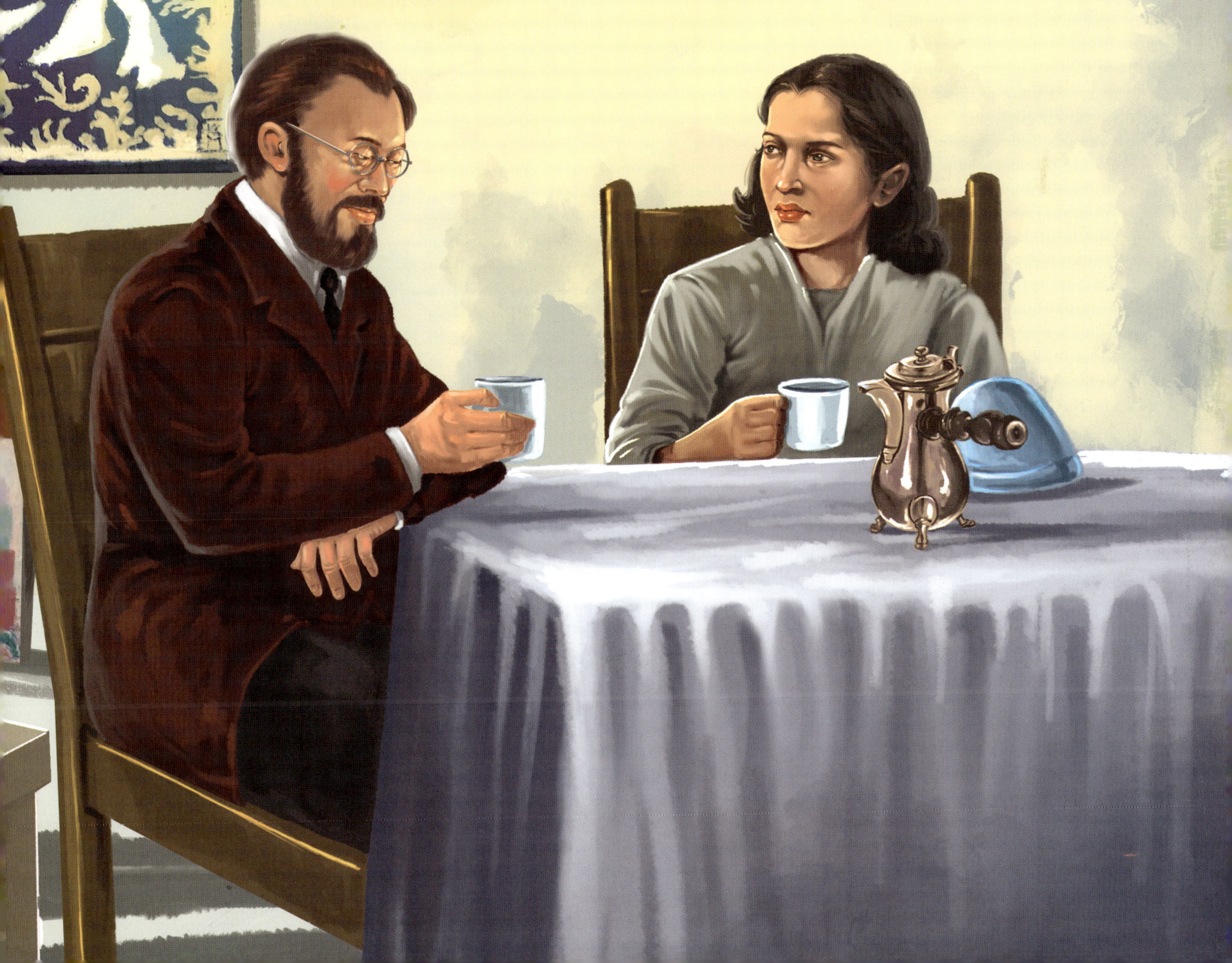

M. Chocolatière was rudely awakened the next morning. Henri opened out the windows of the studio and arranged a book at the far corner. He placed M. Chocolatière on top of the book.

He then lifted red colour out of Miss Paint-box and dabbed it on Mr. Easel.

Henri would stare at Mr. Easel every now and then, he would sometimes smile and sometimes snort with contempt.

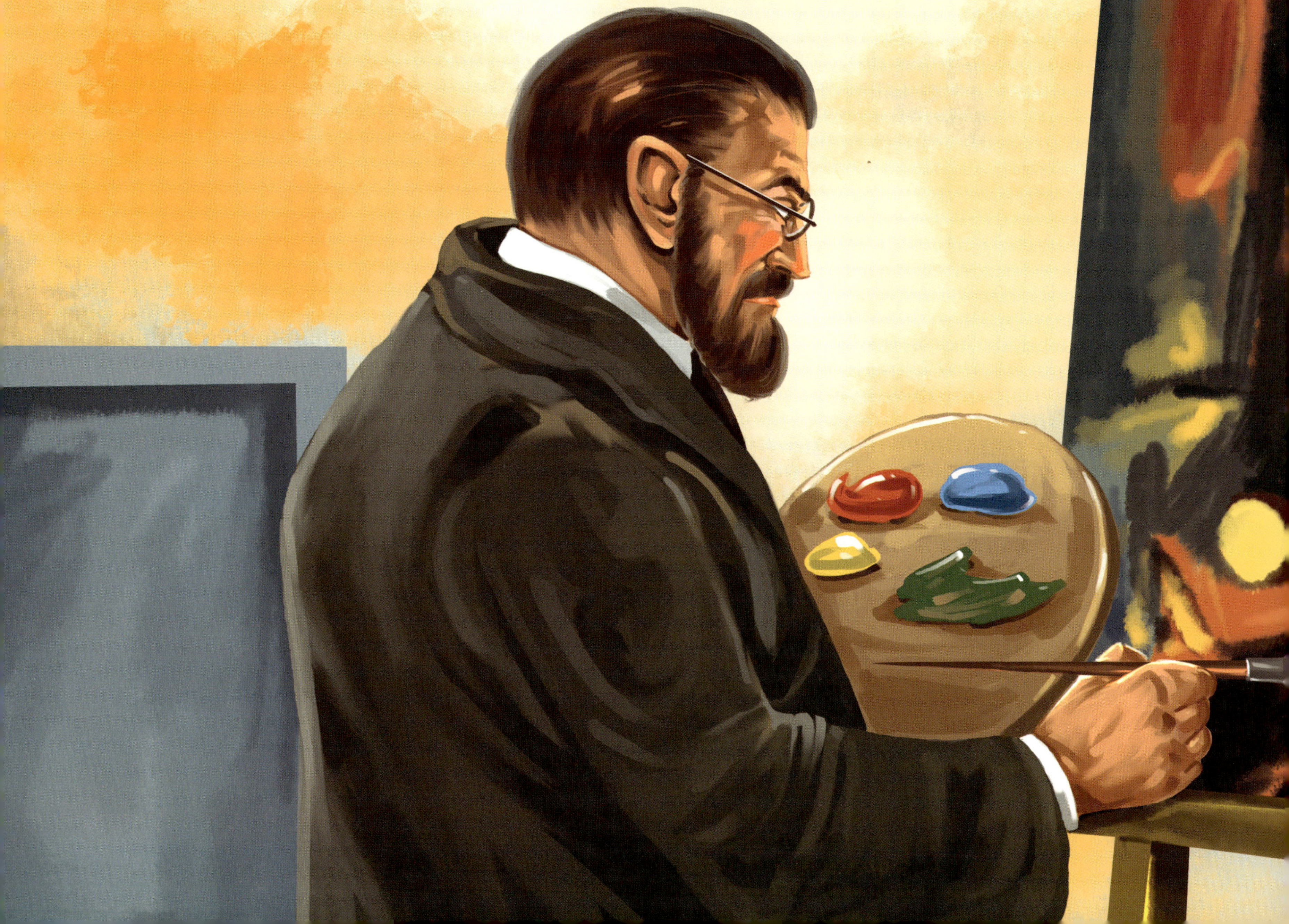

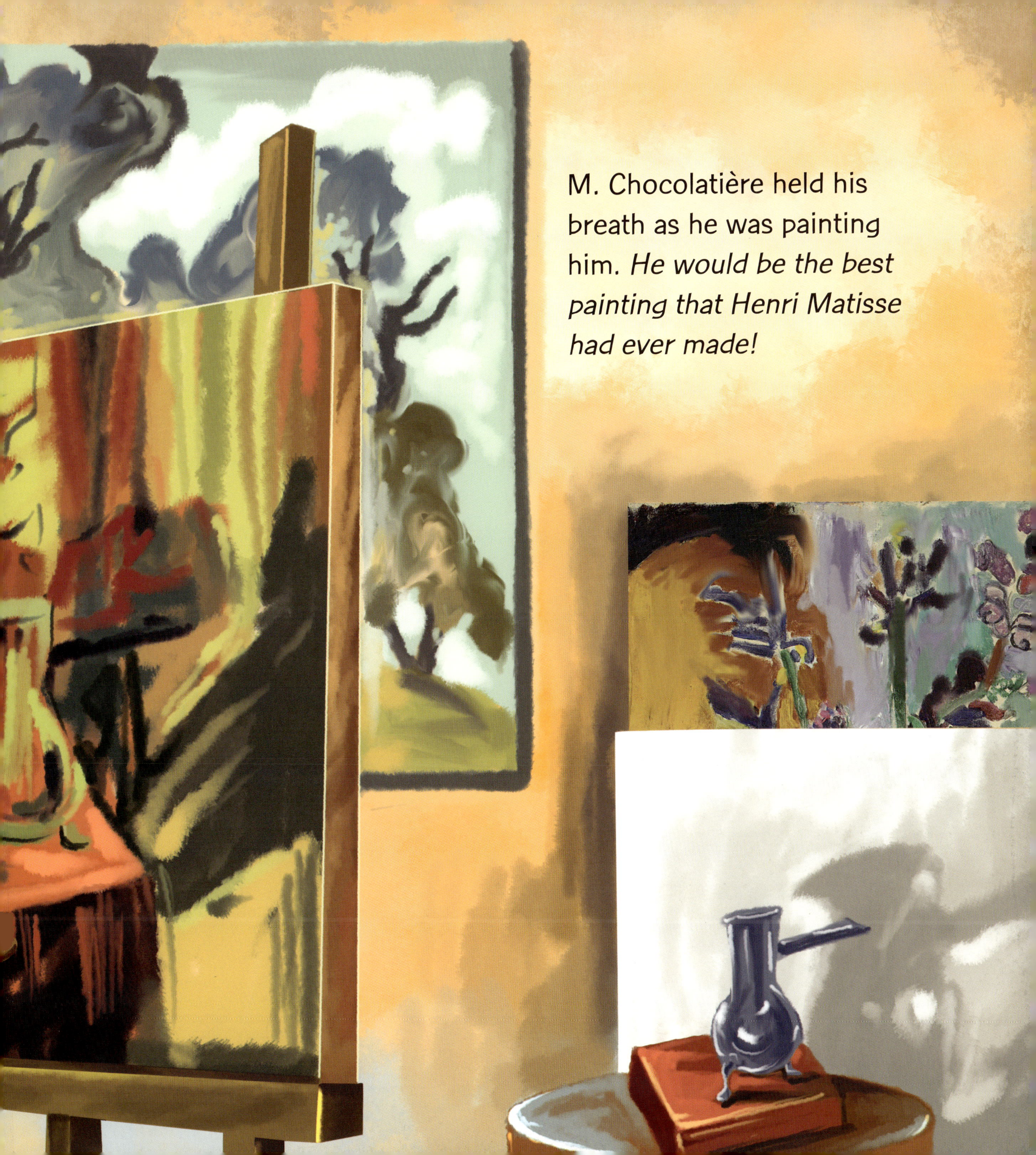

M. Chocolatière held his breath as he was painting him. *He would be the best painting that Henri Matisse had ever made!*

Scritch-scratch. Scritch-scratch.

'Who is this? So early in the morning!' said M. Chocolatière. He saw a young girl bent over the table, pretending to read.

So this was Marguerite. Henri's daughter. Henri carried on painting. 'Stay still girl!' yelled M. Chocolatière. 'We are going to be famous!'

Marguerite giggled. 'Did you just say that we are going to be famous?'

'Look at the way he puts colours, it's brilliant,' said M. Chocolatière. 'Your daddy is Chief of the Fauvists, I heard them talking yesterday while having coffee.'

'What are the Fauvists?' asked Marguerite.

'See, how they use strong colours, not like the ones that the object is made of,' said M. Chocolatière.

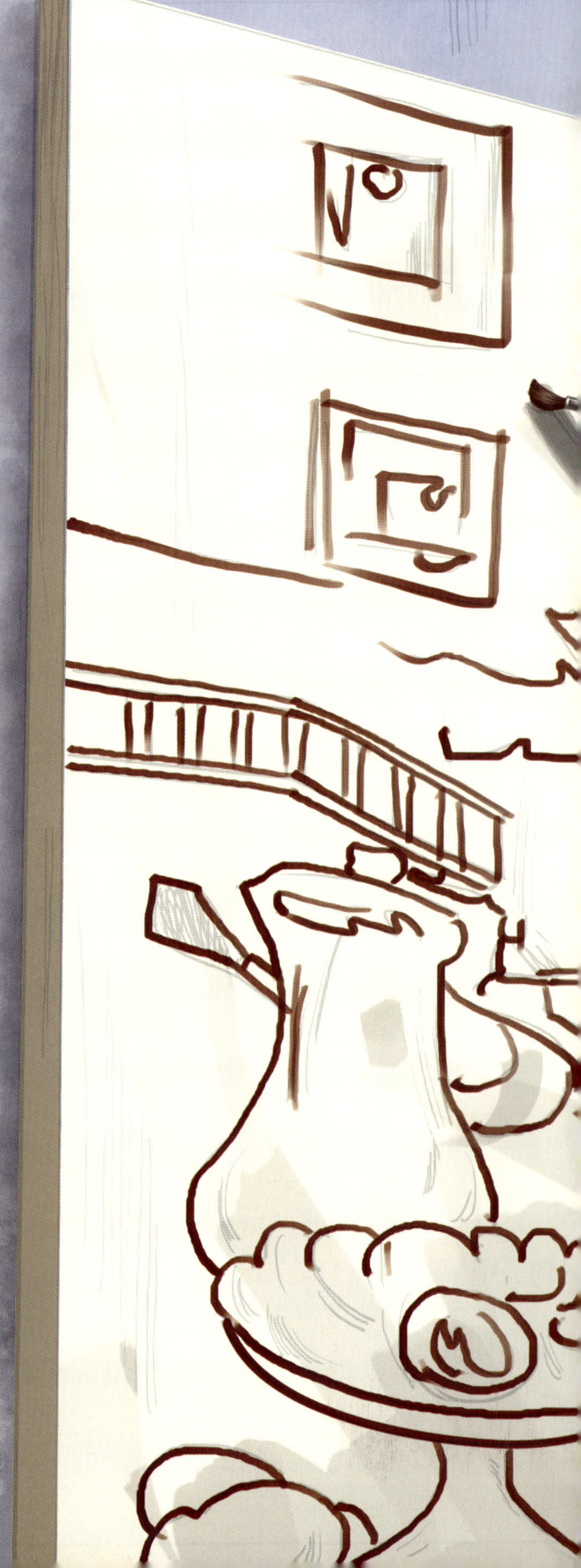

'Oooooh, I see it now,'
said Marguerite.

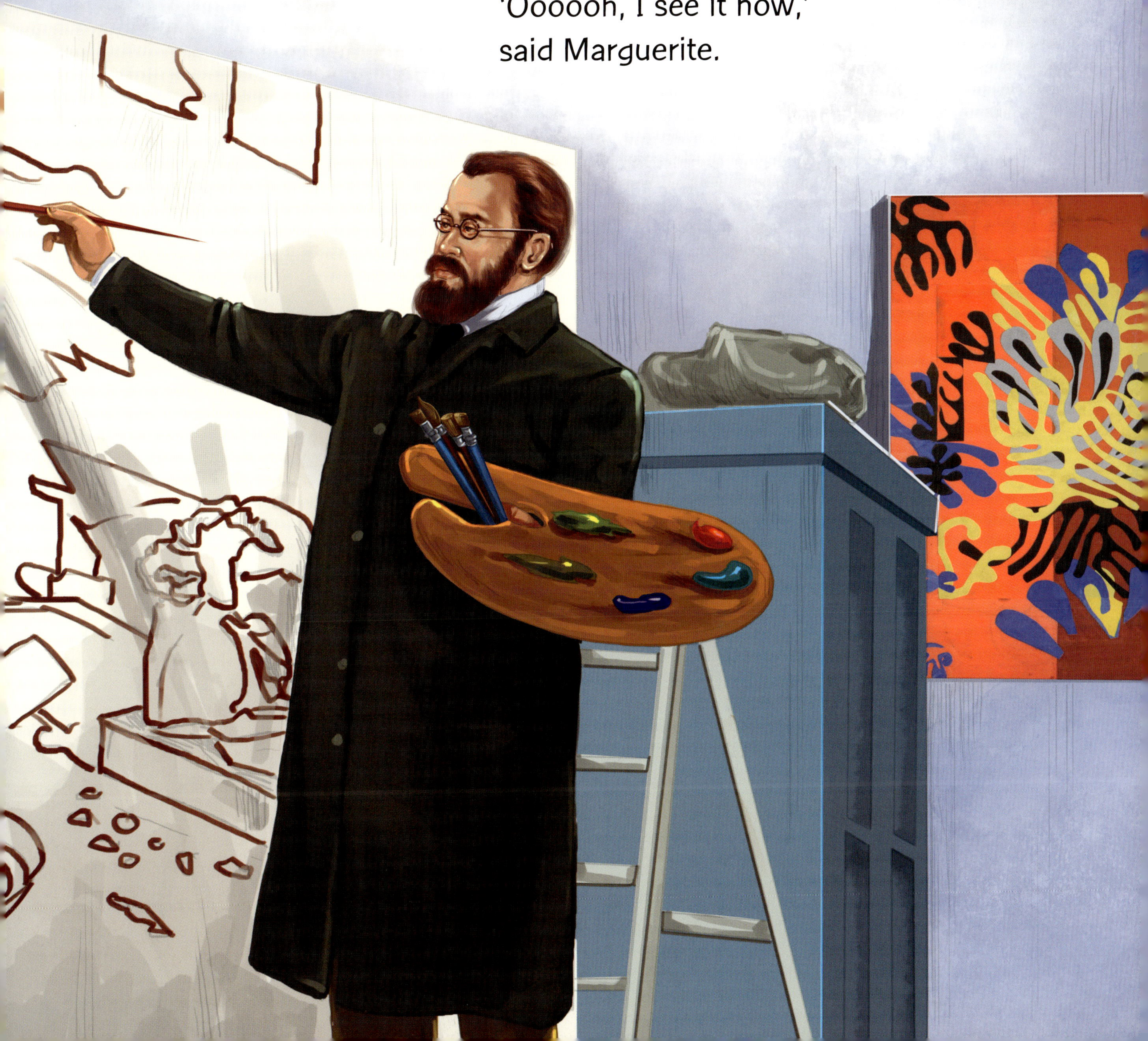

M. Chocolatier was excited as he had never been out of the country. Miss Paint-Box was nervous that she would be sea sick while Mr. Easel had got a fresh new canvas for their journey to Tangier in Morocco.

It was raining in Tangier when they arrived. Henri picked a beautiful bunch of purple irises to paint.

'Ah-choo,' sneezed M. Chocolatière, the damp weather was giving him an awful cold.

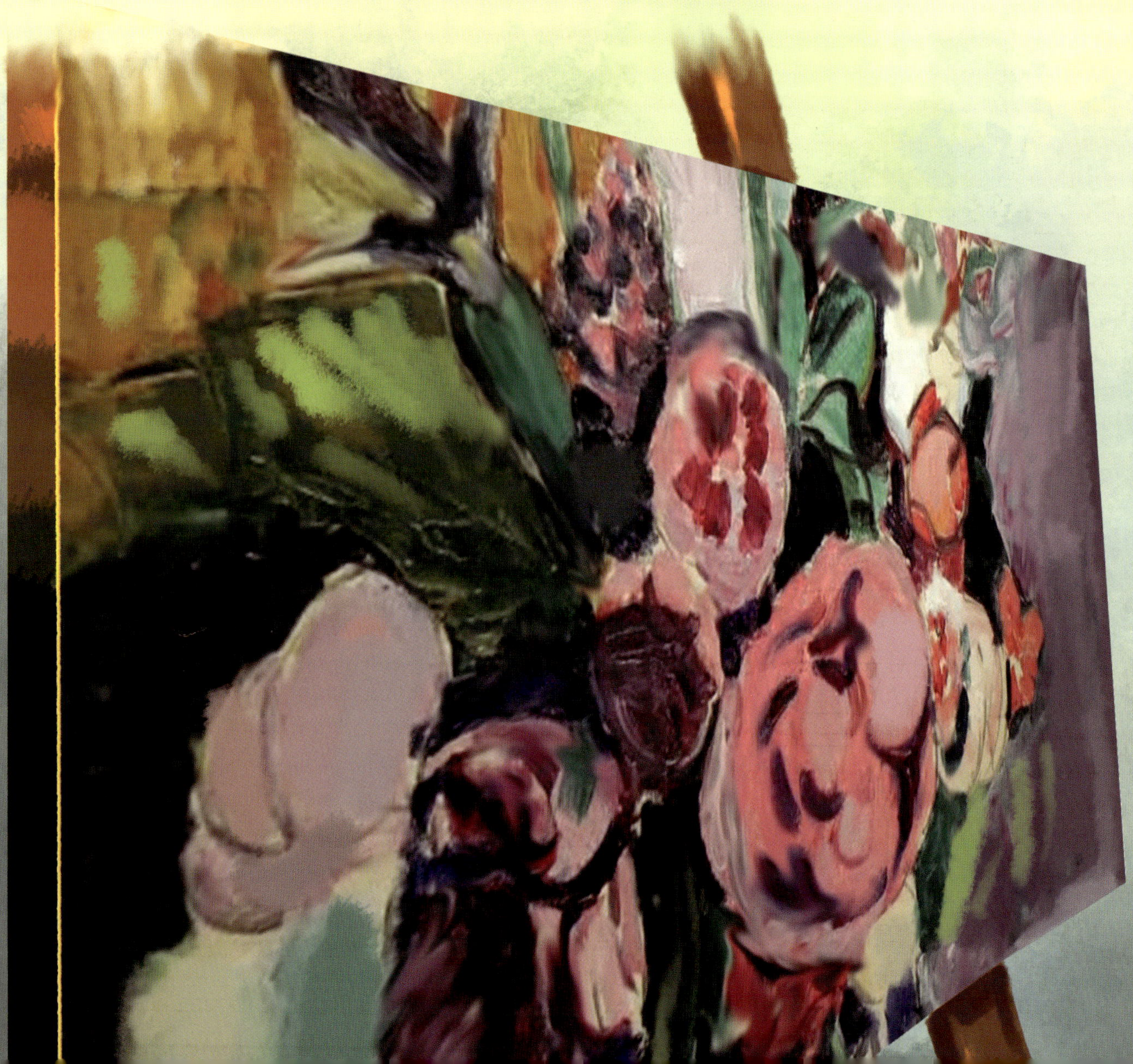

It rained for days and days. Henri missed home. He wrote to Amelie that his objects kept him company. When the rain cleared, the irises took them to the gardens of Villa Brooks. It was a burst of colours they had never seen before.

Henri took one colour after another from Miss Paint-box. 'Colours, they must be thought, dreamed and imagined,' said a delighted Henri. *It was like he had found a whole new palette of colours,* thought M. Chocolatière.

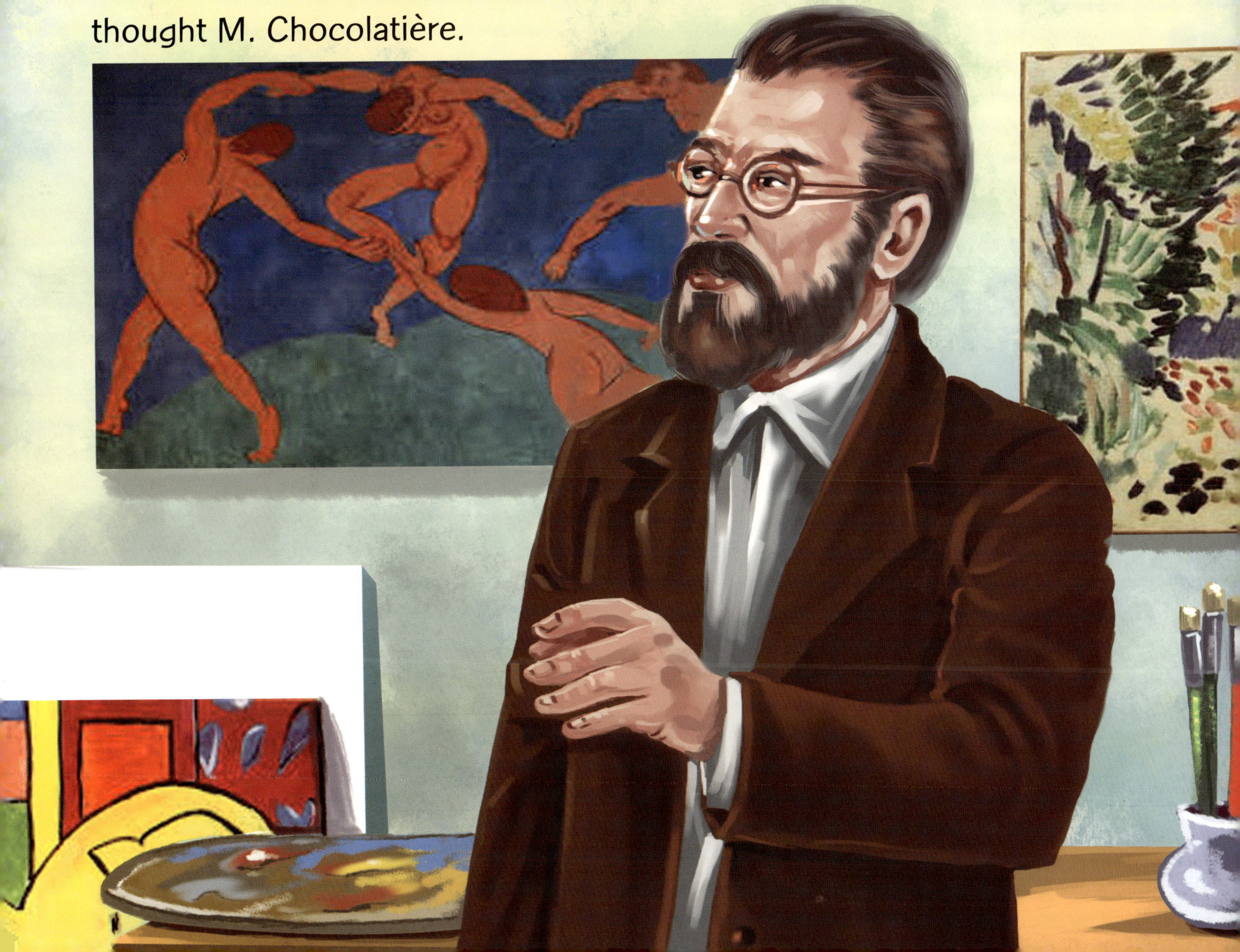

Soon they were back in Paris. M. Chocolatière was nervous as he'd been hearing all the talk about the war. He heard the bombs that night. Rations were being stocked in the house, M. Chocolatière shivered with fright. What if they all got destroyed?

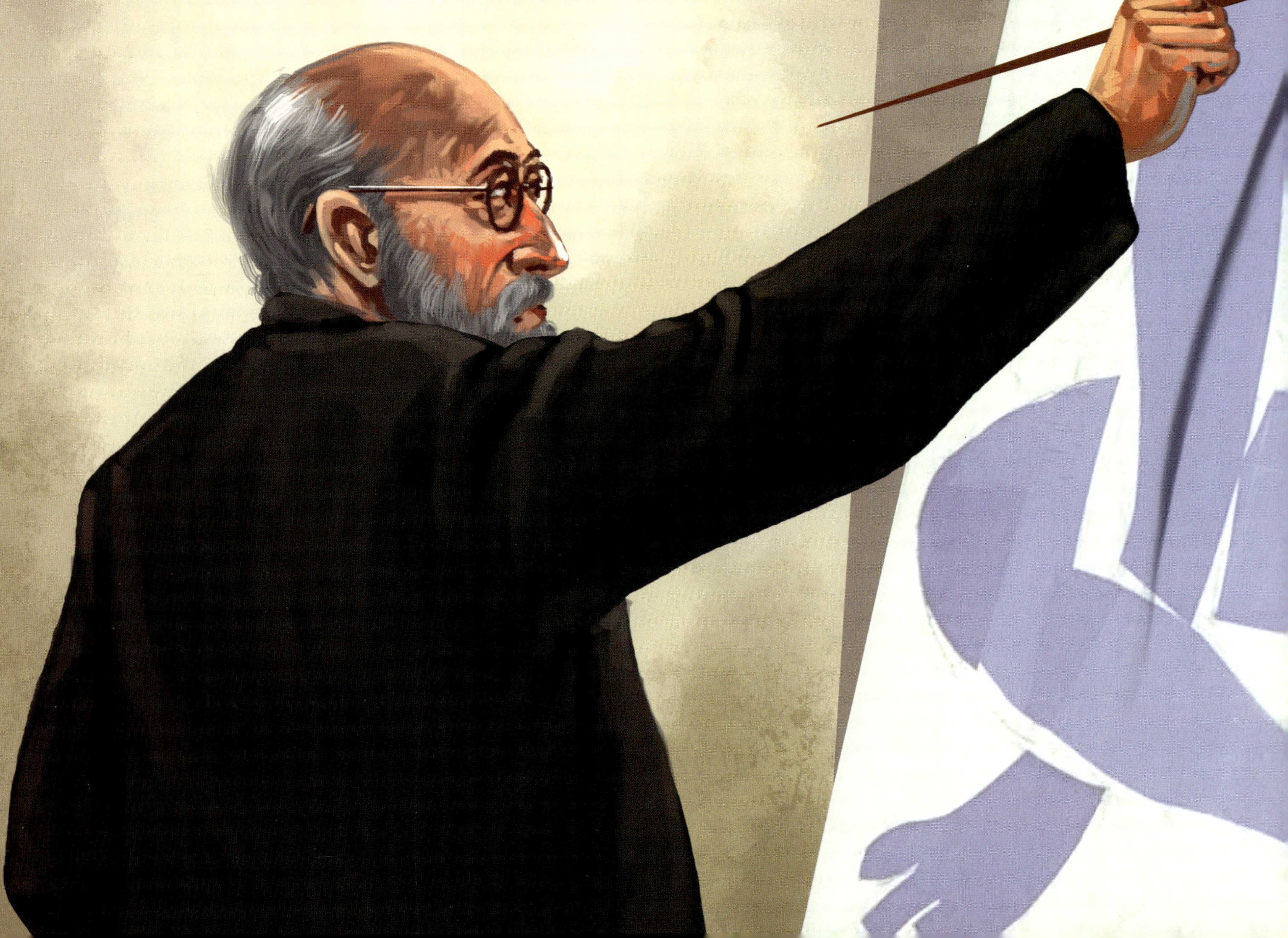

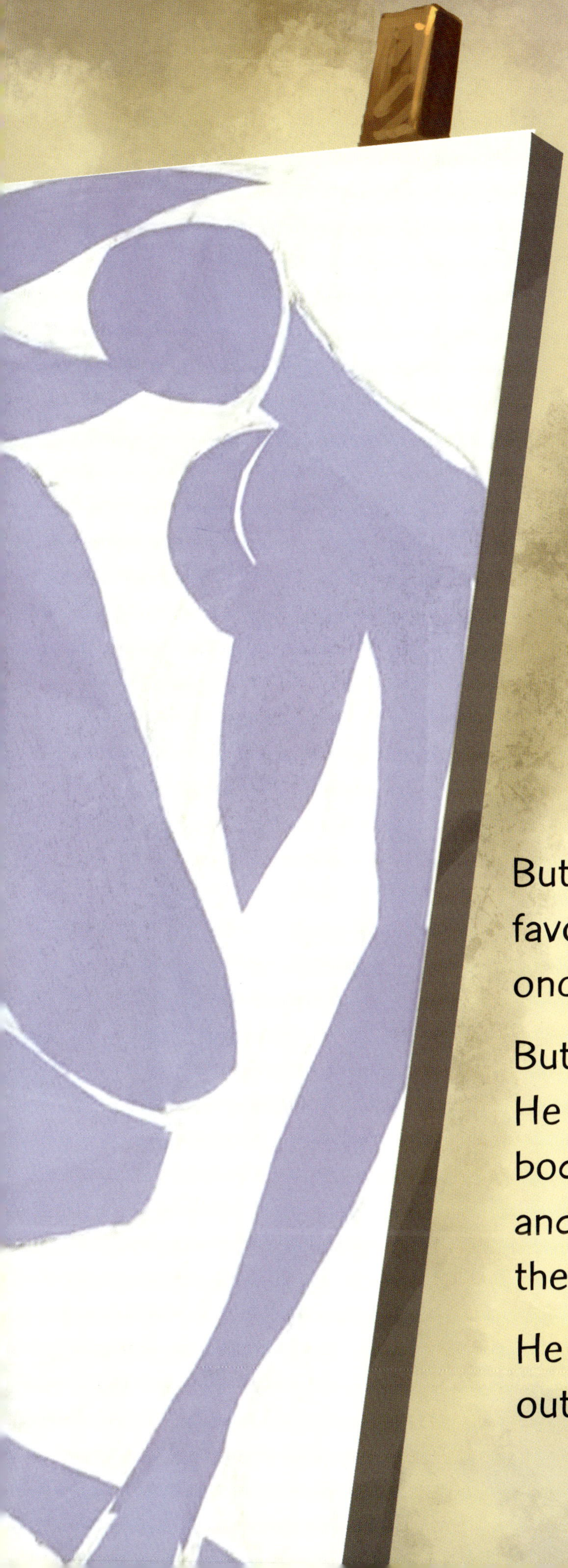

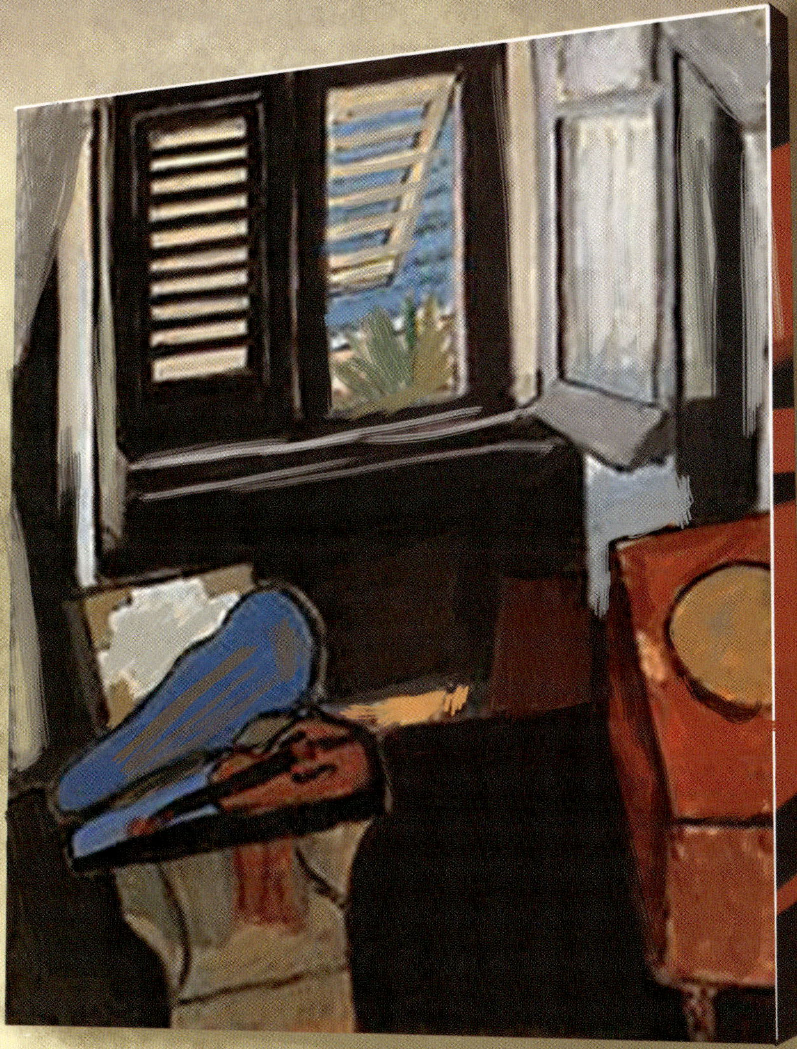

But Henri had a plan. He gathered all his favourite objects and travelled with them once again. This time it was Nice.

But in Nice, Henri forgot about M. Chocolatière. He lay in a corner. M. Chocolatière whose silver body had always been polished, got browner and browner. Days passed, then weeks and then, years.

He saw Henri paint some of the most outstanding works.

When Henri returned home he fell out of love with Amelie. Every day they would be fighting about who would get what. Amelie left the house, which made M. Chocolatière very sad. He couldn't bear to see Henri, now with white hair and wrinkled hands.

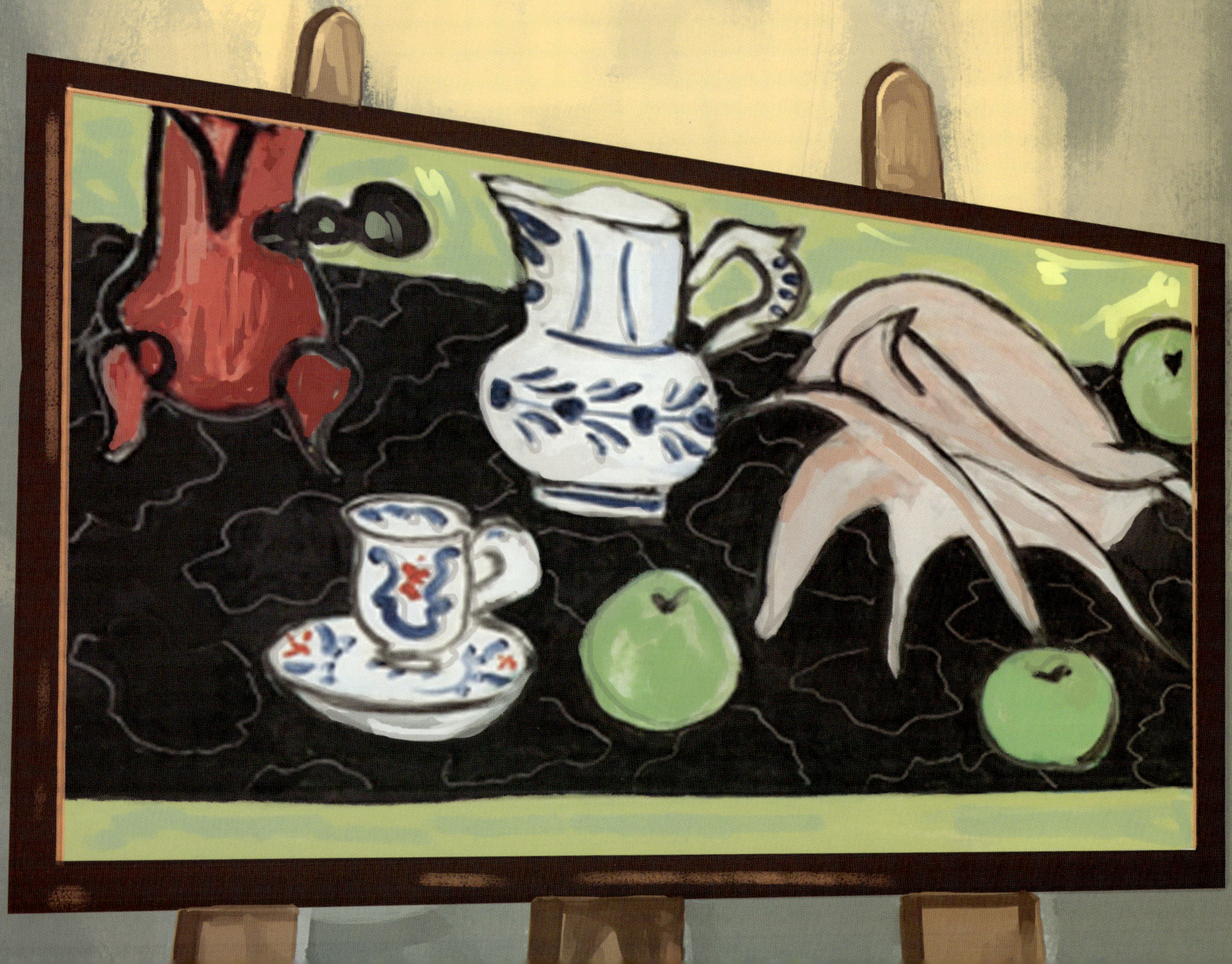

'Ah my friend, I've been looking for you,' said Henri.

Really? After thirty years, Henri had remembered him?

'I am going to make a cut out of you,' said Henri.

Once again M. Chocolatière was polished, he shone like a newborn baby and sat happily on Henri's bedside table.

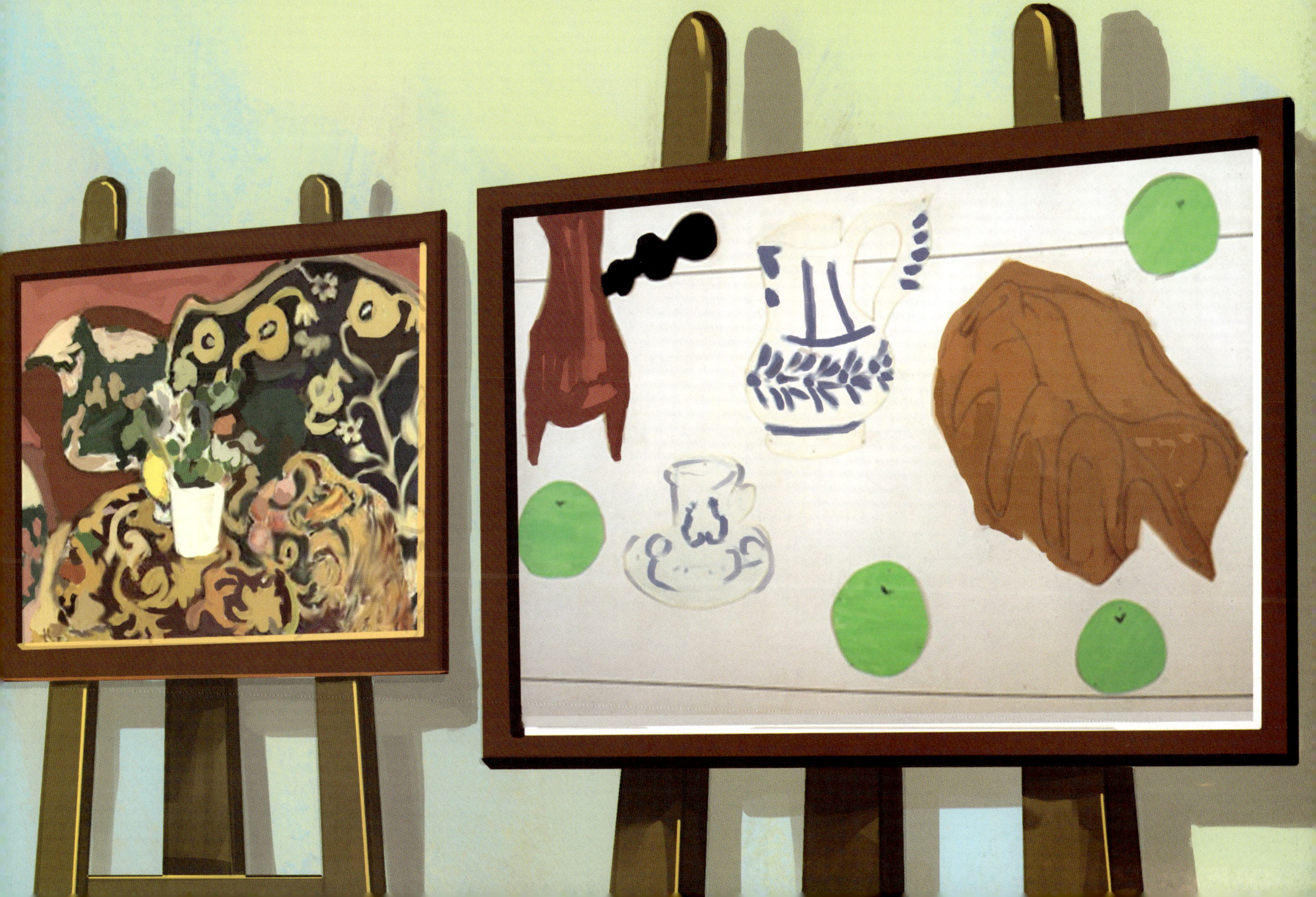

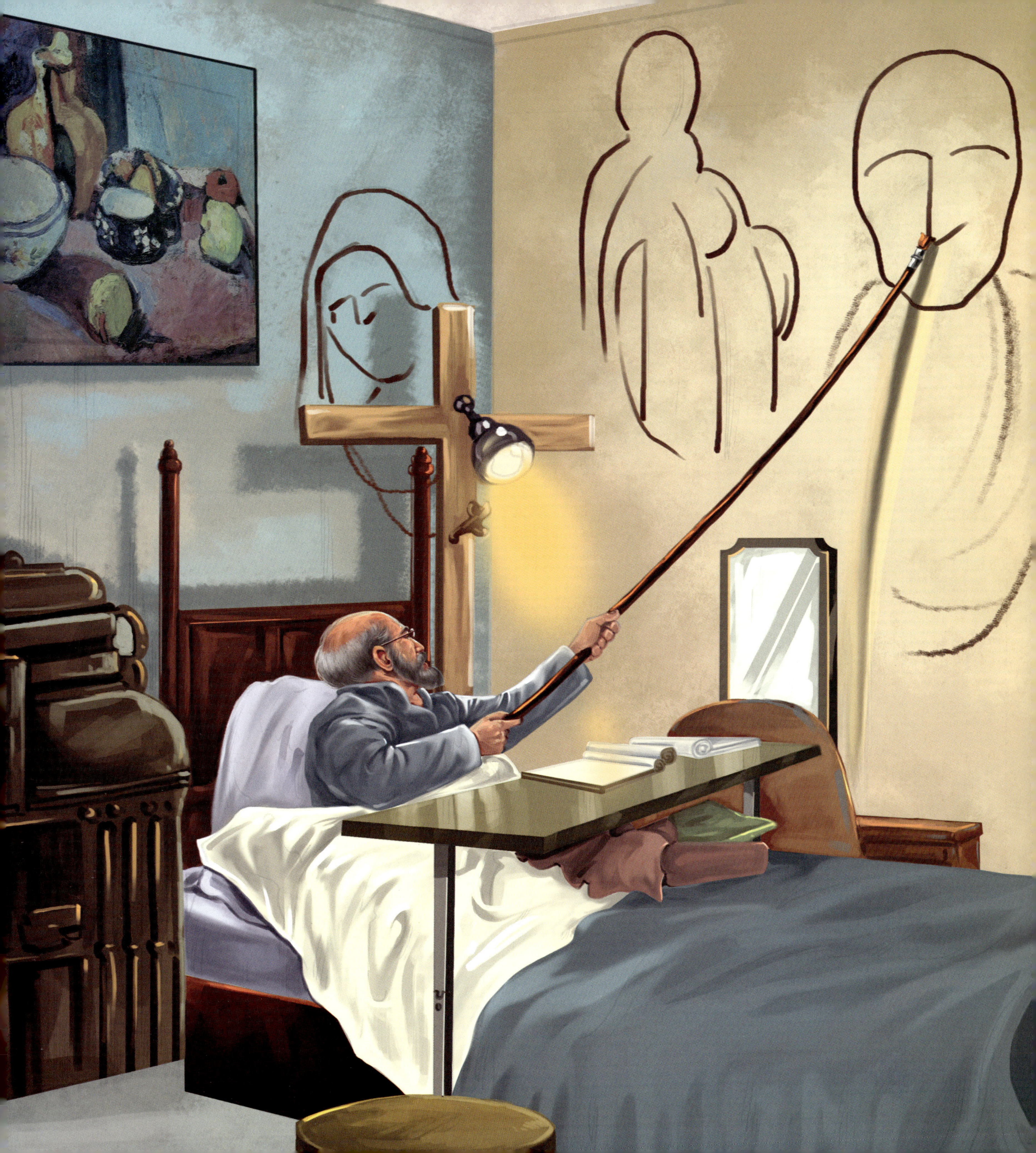

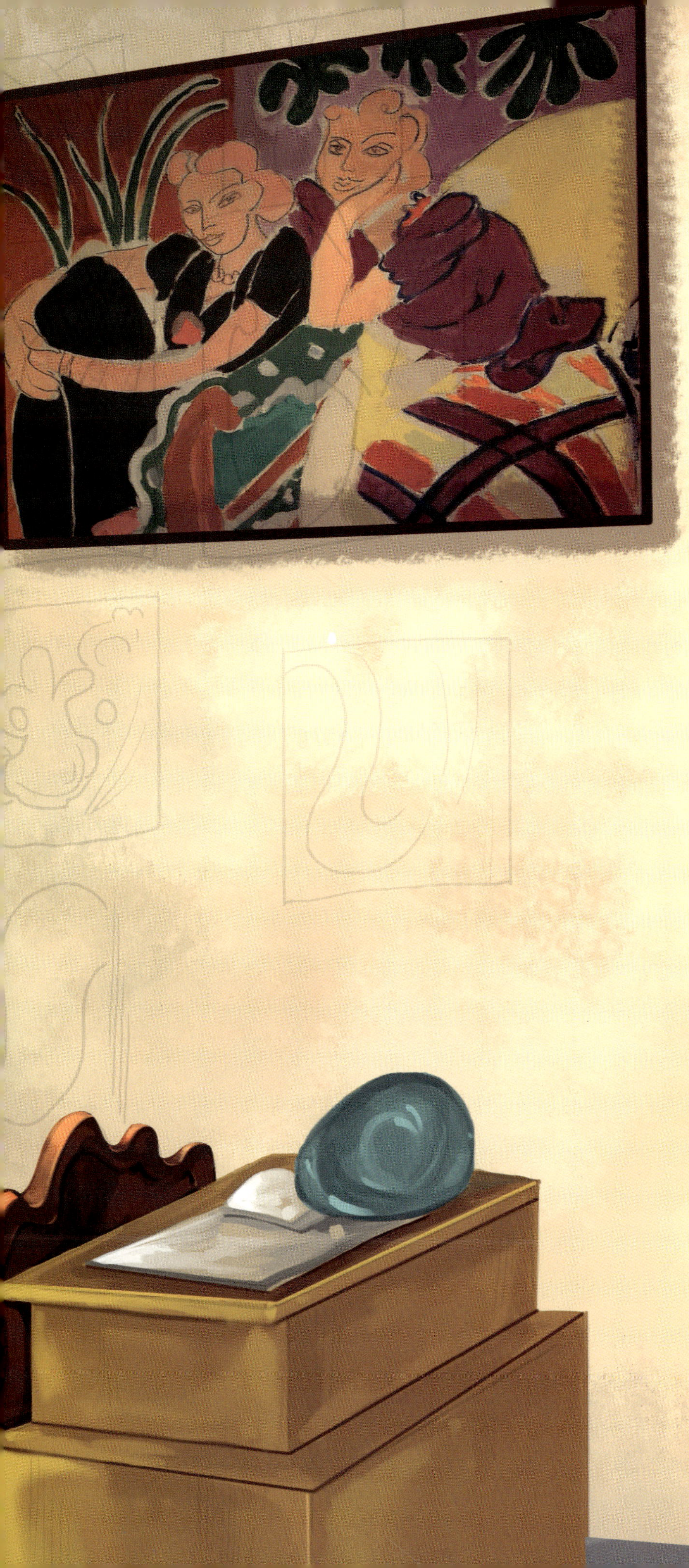

M. Chocolatière, Miss Paint-box and Mr. Easel took turns looking after Henri as he grew older and frailer. There were days when he couldn't move out of his bed but he never stopped creating. He would sketch the walls of his room for the cut-outs that had become his passion, or spend weeks cutting paper to make the most fabulous paper paintings. M. Chocolatière whistled as he knew he would be famous one day through Henri's paintings.

Henri Matisse was born in Le Cateau-Cambrésis, Nord, France in 1869.

At 20 years of age he had an attack of appendicitis when his mother gave him a box of paints that started his journey as an artist.

He studied in Paris at the Academie Julian and then at Ecole des Beaux-Arts in 1891.

Matisse loved to experiment with new kinds of brush work. His travels to North Africa and his fascination with light and composition gave his style a unique pictorial language.

He is remembered for his Favuist (from the French word 'fauve' that signifies 'wild beast') technique that used bright colours and energetic brushwork in the early 1900s.

Matisse married Amelie Noellie Parayre in 1989 and had two sons with her. He also raised Marguerite, his daughter from a model who used to work for him.

In 1939, he divorced Amelie and partnered with Lydia Delectorskaya who handled his art-related work.

In 1925, he was awarded the French Legion of Honor, the highest decoration in France.

He died at the age of 84 in Nice, France.

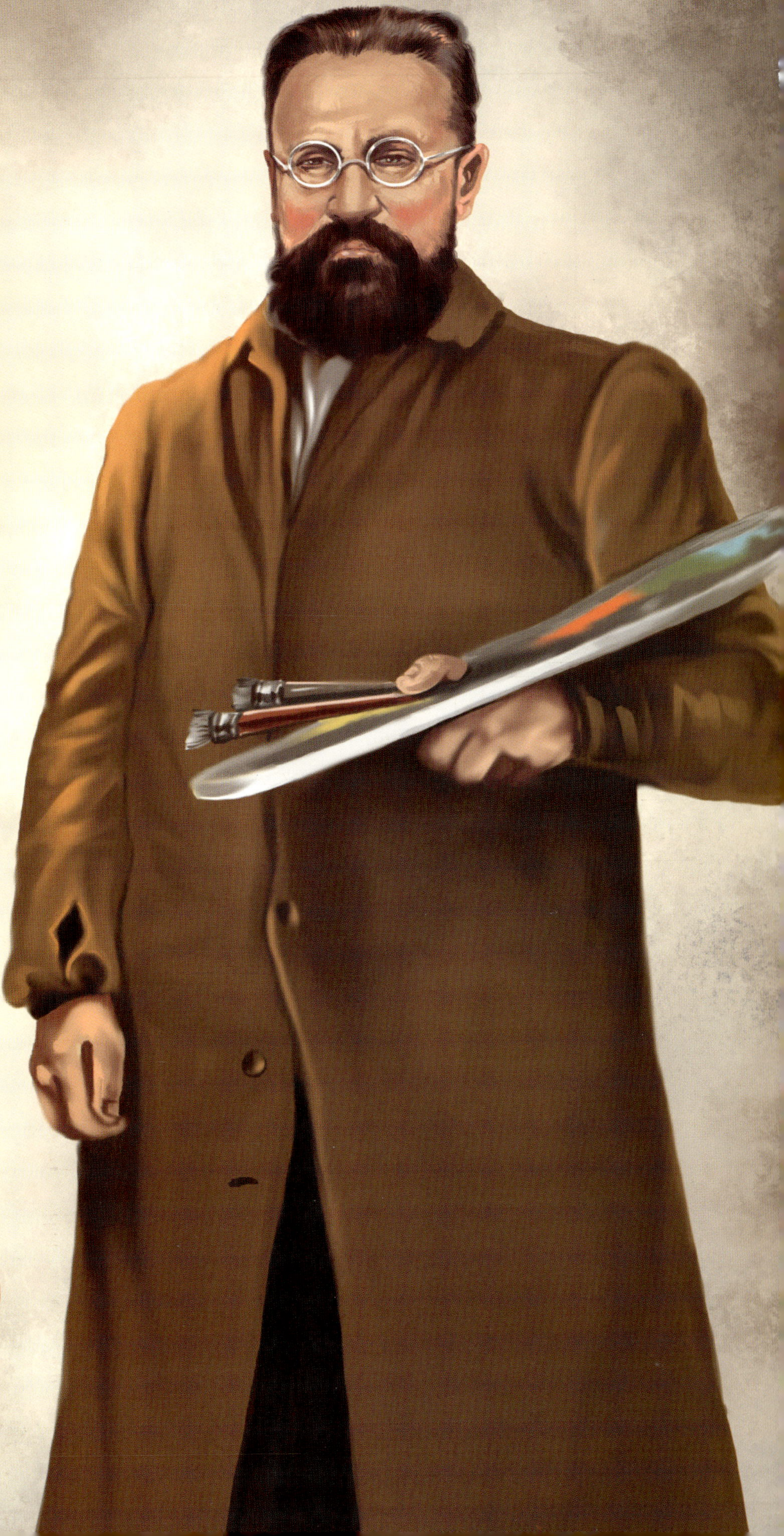